Little Piggy's Big Day

by Violet Findley
illustrated by Kelly Kennedy

SCHOLASTIC INC.

New York • Toronto • London • Auckland • Sydney
Mexico City • New Delhi • Hong Kong • Buenos Aires

Designed by Maria Lilja
ISBN-13: 978-0-545-08702-5 • ISBN-10: 0-545-08702-3

First printing, October 2008

12 11 10 9 8 7 6 5 4 3 2 1 8 9 10 11 12 13/0

Building Vocabulary With This Book

This book contains eight key words that are important for all children to know. Read the story straight through for enjoyment. Then read it again, pausing to define and discuss each key word. Follow-up the tale with the fun activities on pages 14–16. When you're done, celebrate—kids will have added eight great words to their vocabularies!

This little piggy closed her front door.
She stepped outside—time to explore!

KEY WORD: neighbor

Simple Definition: someone who lives nearby

Sample Sentence: My *neighbor*, Lynn, lives right next door.

She waved to her **neighbor**, Larry Moo.
He lived next door. His house was blue.

KEY WORD: **diner**

Simple Definition: a restaurant that has all kinds of food

Sample Sentence: The *diner* on Main Street serves yummy soup and pie.

She walked 'round the corner and into a **diner**.
The food was delicious. It couldn't be finer!

KEY WORD: **museum**

Simple Definition: a place where art, history, or science objects are displayed

Sample Sentence: Let's go to the *museum* and look at the dinosaur bones.

Then, to the **museum** she skipped with glee.
There was so much excellent art to see!

KEY WORD: **browse**

Simple Definition: to look at a lot of different things

Sample Sentence: I like to *browse* in the bookstore and pick a book that looks good.

A fancy shop was right next door.
It was fun to **browse** around the store!

What did she do right after that?
This little piggy put on her new hat!

KEY WORD: pharmacy

Simple Definition: a drugstore, where you can buy medicine and other things

Sample Sentence: Dad bought me some cough drops at the *pharmacy* to make my sore throat feel better.

The **pharmacy** was piggy's next stop.
She bought pink soap and a lime lollipop.

KEY WORD: **theater**

Simple Definition: a building where movies or plays are shown

Sample Sentence: We went to a big *theater* to see a play called *The King and I.*

She dashed to the **theater** and sat in a seat.
Movies and treats just cannot be beat!

KEY WORD: borrow

Simple Definition: to use something that doesn't belong to you, then give it back

Sample Sentence: Lynn likes to *borrow* her mom's sparkly shoes to play dress-up.

The library was near and she had a card.
Which book should she **borrow**? Picking was hard!

KEY WORD: mayor

Simple Definition: the leader of a town or city

Sample Sentence: The *mayor* of our city passed a law that said everyone has to recycle their newspapers.

She went to the park. Wow, it was pretty!
The **mayor** was there. He's head of the city!

Last but not least, she sat under a tree.
Then, she ran home—*wee, wee, wee*!

Exploring the neighborhood was lots of fun.
But this little piggy's big day is done.

Meaning Match

neighborhood words

Listen to the definition. Then go to the WORD CHEST and find a vocabulary word that matches it.

1. someone who lives nearby
2. a place where art, history, or science objects are displayed
3. a building where movies or plays are shown
4. using something that doesn't belong to you, then giving it back
5. a drugstore
6. to look at a lot of different things
7. a restaurant that has all kinds of food
8. the leader of a town or city

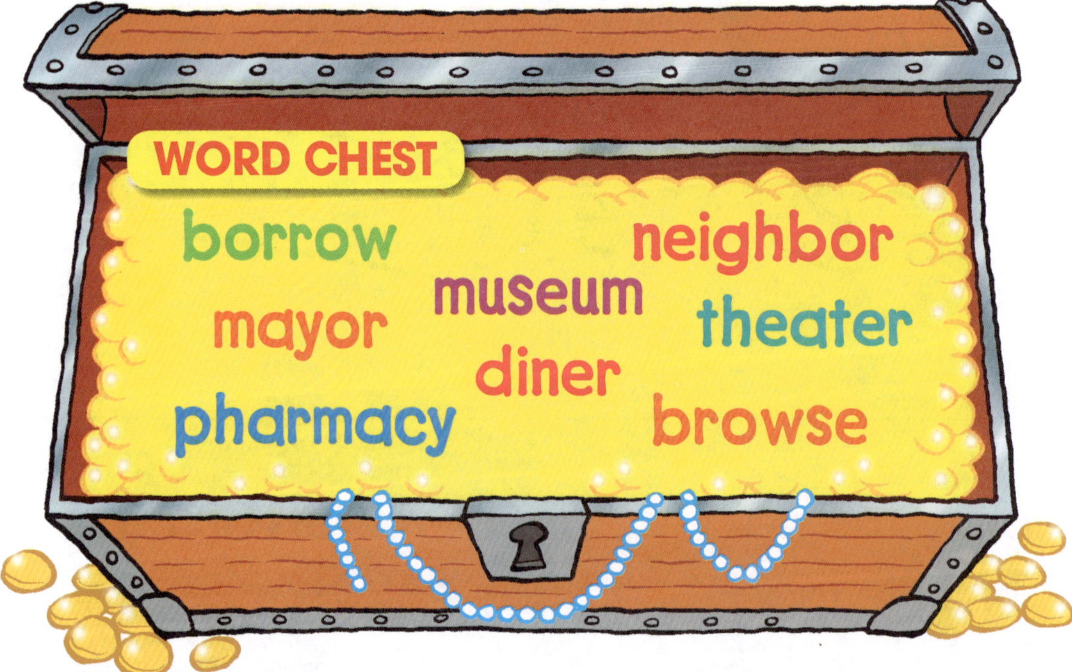

Answers: 1. neighbor 2. museum 3. theater 4. borrow 5. pharmacy 6. browse 7. diner 8. mayor

Vocabulary Fill-ins

neighborhood words

Listen to the sentence. Then go to the WORD BOX and find the best word to fill in the blank.

WORD BOX

neighbor	mayor	diner	borrow
pharmacy	browse	theater	museum

1. Can I __________ your markers to make a picture?
2. When I was sick, my mom bought me medicine at the __________.
3. Joan likes to __________ in toy stores.
4. Mary loves to go to the __________ and eat a big stack of pancakes and a bowl of soup!
5. The __________ is giving a speech today about ways to improve our city.
6. We went to the __________ and looked at the mummies and old pots.
7. My friend Jordan lives next door. He is my __________.
8. Hooray, Dad said we could get red licorice at the movie __________!

Answers: 1. borrow 2. pharmacy 3. browse 4. diner 5. mayor 6. museum 7. neighbor 8. theater

Vocabulary Questions

neighborhood words

Listen to the question. Think about it. Then answer.

1. Who are your **neighbors**? Share a fact about each one.
2. Have you ever been to a **museum**? What is your favorite thing to look at?
3. Pretend you are going to go to a **diner** for dinner. What will you order?
4. Do you like to **borrow** things from other people? What are some good rules for borrowing things?
5. What can you buy at a **pharmacy**? Make a list.
6. Have you ever been to a **movie** theater? What is the best movie you ever saw?
7. Where do you like to **browse**? What do you like to look at?
8. Do you know the name of the **mayor** of your city or town? What do you know about him or her?

Extra: Can you think of some more neighborhood words? Make a list.